EntrepreFriendships™

Step-by-Step Guide to Make More Meaningful
Connections, Earn Greater Business Opportunities,
and Develop Real Business Relationships

Monique Melton

www.moniquemelton.com
hello@moniiquemelton.com

Disclaimer: This book is not intended as a substitute for medical, mental,
spiritual, or legal advice. Readers should use the information within this book at
their own discretion.

Acknowledgments

There are so many people who pour into me and support me, and I am so grateful for that. I want to give a special thank you to God, my incredibly supportive husband, my two gorgeous-charming children, my family, my sassy-soul sisters (you know exactly who you are) and amazing friends, and incredible business connections. I want to specifically thank one of my incredible clients and friends, who inspired this book. I offered the material here to her team during a two-hour training and she loved it. I told her I would send her the resource, and as I sat down to spruce it up, I decided to turn it into a book. Many thanks to you, Carrie Polk, owner of Carrie Polk Insurance Agency.

Contents

The image on the cover is representative of this scripture:

A person standing alone can be attacked and defeated, but two can stand back-to-back and conquer. Three are even better, for a triple-braided cord is not easily broken.

- Ecclesiastes 4:12 (NLT)

Introduction

❤

When you decided to start your business did you say, "I want to be lonely and isolated, and feel like no one really understands or supports me?"

I'm willing to bet my favorite pink pumps that you didn't say that at all. When you decided to take your creative talent, beautiful passion, devoted purpose, and strong commitment to make a difference in your community, I'm sure you didn't expect or anticipate it to be such an overwhelming and lonely experience. You probably didn't imagine the many days of being behind your computer working so hard to connect with people, all while feeling even more disconnected. You believe in what you're doing and you knew it would take hard work, so you were willing to trade lunches with friends for awkward networking events with strangers. You were willing to miss a date night or two in exchange for a really boring and shallow lunch date. You were willing to avoid splurging on those new shoes because you wanted to make sure you paid your monthly dues to that networking organization. You were willing to do all of this because you hoped it would help you make connections and build business relationships. But what happened instead? Something you didn't expect.

You went to the networking event and barely had any meaningful conversation, left feeling like it was a waste of your time, and wondered if you would even bother to go the next time.

You went to the lunch meeting and talked about shallow and surface topics while resisting the urge to check your email or Facebook updates—anything to distract you from the fact that you were having a really boring time. You walked away wondering what just happened and thinking about how you would have been better off responding to those emails you've been meaning to get to all week, rather than spending an hour having a conversation about...well, you don't even remember what it was about.

You avoided buying the new shoes (even though you really needed another really fly pair of pumps—can never have enough of those!) so you could pay your membership dues to that organization that everyone seemed to suggest that you join, but no one seems to be really having a great time or getting a whole lot out of the group.

You did all of these things and more with great intentions, yet you've found yourself in a place you didn't expect: a place of feeling disengaged and lonely.

You're doing the right things, but can't seem to figure out why you're not meeting and connecting with the right people. And over time you find yourself feeling alone—lonely and isolated—because you just can't seem to get in a good and exciting groove of connecting with people in a real and meaningful way. And although you know that building connections and making business relationships are important, you just can't seem to figure out how to do it without feeling fake and cheesy.

Or maybe you're not getting out there and meeting people because you're crippled with fear and have so much uncertainty about building business relationships that you don't even bother with it at all. Yet you know you should. It really doesn't matter if you've tried and haven't succeeded or if you haven't tried at all; the truth is building relationships is a cornerstone to building a great business and having a great presence in your community—online and offline.

Fix the Signals: Untangle the Mixed Messages About Business Relationships

♥

We are made to connect and be in relationships with others. We are made to be in close connection and commune with all sorts of people, and this is especially true for business. But somehow in the effort to build relationships and build our brands, the signals get crossed and things just don't seem to light up the way that you desire.

It doesn't help that there are so many mixed signals about building business relationships. Some say business is cut-throat, which may lead you to think twice about building business relationships. Who wants to be in a relationship with someone they feel has the intention or at least the capability of stabbing them in the back at the first chance? That's just downright scary, and if you fear people doing this, I don't blame you for staying far, far away. Others say "community over competition," which sounds great on the surface, but does it mean you have to forsake your business and your brand's viability for the sake of community? I don't think so; there's a place for both. And then you hear that you shouldn't mix business with pleasure.

You also hear that building business relationships is really important, but you don't hear a lot of people sharing with you how to go about doing it.

There's no wonder you find yourself afraid of backstabbers, unsure how far to take this whole community notion and uncertain how to actually build business relationships. There's a lot of misinformation and surface information out there that leaves you still coming up short when it comes to knowing how to build business relationships. With the lack of information and the crossed signals, it's really hard to know where and how to start, especially for those who are naturally shy or introverted. (This explains why so many people find networking to be so uncomfortable and dreadful.) But it doesn't have to be like this. You don't have to be lonely and isolated while you build your business. You don't have to always worry about someone stabbing you in the back. You do have to be smart, though, because there are those backstabbers out there. (Insert the tune of that famous song about people smiling in your face, but all the while they're trying to take your place; they're backstabbers—thank you, Mom and Dad, for exposing me to such great music.) And you don't have to forsake your business growth and development in the pursuit of building community, because there's a place for both business growth and healthy and supportive real community.

You can build really great business relationships. You can understand the process and navigate it with confidence.

What if all you were missing were the steps to actually make it happen?

Dinner for Two: Know the Ingredients and the Recipe for Building Business Relationships

❤

Have you ever dined at a really great restaurant, had the most amazing meal, and then tried to re-create it at home, only to find it doesn't turn out the same—not even close? You had all of the ingredients. At least you thought you did, but something was missing. The recipe—the steps. Once you laid eyes on the recipe you not only realized that you missed some key steps, but you missed some key ingredients. So you try it again, this time following the recipe, and the meal turns out perfect. All hope is restored and you've regained confidence in yourself to actually accomplish something really great.

What if your strategy to building business relationships and EntrepreFriendships is missing some key steps and key ingredients? What if once you take a look at the steps, you realize what was missing, and then you try it with the new steps and ingredients, and amazingness happens?

What if I told you that I believe that amazingness is waiting for you? You just need the right ingredients and the right steps.

The recipe and the ingredients are simple, and in this book I share both with you. But it really all sums up to this: Learn how to build real community and support and serve others, but in a way in which everyone wins.

In this book, I show you step-by-step how to build relationships that serve everyone well. That means the relationships are designed to be supportive and beneficial for you, the other person, and the community you serve. Sound simple enough? With this book you'll have practical and clear direction on what it takes to create and build real business relationships and EntrepreFriendships.

EntrepreFriendships Defined—and Why You Need Them

♥

Business relationships and EntrepreFriendships are both important to business growth and development, but they are not the same. A business relationship tends to be more casual and is not necessarily mutually beneficial. An EntrepreFriendship is a lot more intentional and involved, with both parties committed to supporting and being of service to one another. A business relationship can do many of the things that an EntrepreFriendship can do, however an EntrepreFriendship is much more consistent, involved, and intentional. (The different types of business relationships are explained later in the book in Step 4.)

The harsh reality is that entrepreneurship has the potential to be very lonely. There are days when you may feel like you're all alone and no one really understands, or even cares, about what you're going through. This is one very critical reason for establishing business relationships and especially EntrepreFriendships.

An EntrepreFriendship can come along during those times to remind you that you're not alone and that someone really does care. But an EntrepreFriend is more than a cheerleader or a great encourager. An EntrepreFriend can be a key player in growing your business. They can be someone that you work with on projects, collaborations, and joint ventures. An EntrepreFriend can also be a really great strategic partner and a wonderful advocate. You two share referrals and business opportunities to support and help one another grow.

An EntrepreFriend will connect you with their connections and circle of influencers, and you will do the same for them. Over time, as you continue to grow and develop business relationships and new EntrepreFriendships, your network grows. Having a healthy-sized network is one of the often-unspoken rules of business growth and development.

Simply put, an EntrepreFriendship will help you and your business grow, and will help you feel accountable, supported, and cared for—all while giving you access to new networks, connections, and platforms to grow your brand and increase your brand awareness in the community. An EntrepreFriendship is like a business best friend or a really great musical collaboration in that when it comes together awesomeness happens. Think about all of the music duos and collaborations we see. Think about the opening acts at concerts that give the new artist a chance to reach an already-established platform and targeted community. Those opportunities are priceless and really propel a brand forward.

EntrepreFriendships can also make your marketing efforts work more effectively. You need not take a casual or haphazard approach to developing building relationships, especially EntrepreFriendships. Building business relationships and EntrepreFriendships can help you and your business grow to new levels, can help you surpass your goals, and can also give you new opportunities to support and serve others in a more consistent and meaningful way, which is very fulfilling. Relationship building needs to take priority in your business. In fact, building business relationships and EntrepreFriendships really needs to be one of the pillars of building your brand and serving your community. But it's not just about what relationships can do for you; of course it's also about what you can do for them.

Supporting and serving others are what real community is all about. They're what real marketing is all about. Marketing is about relationships, and healthy relationships grow and blossom when all parties make a commitment to support and serve one another as best they can. In business relationships, especially EntrepreFriendships, that means encouraging one another; referring business to one another; spreading the word about each other's events, products, and services; sharing collaboration opportunities with one another; and giving one another a chance to be introduced to your platform and community.

Business relationships and EntrepreFriendships make for healthier businesses and thriving communities. And they aren't for just those sassy, bold women who walk in the room with big hair, sequin tops, and shiny accessories and who can somehow work the room like a superstar. (Yes, I just described myself.) Business relationships and EntrepreFriendships are not just for those women, but instead they really can be for anyone willing to work to create and nurture them. That's why I wrote this book: to not only tell you why you need business relationships and EntrepreFriendships, but how to actually create, build, and nurture them. I love showing you how; it's the how that really makes the difference.

I Know What You're Thinking—and This Is Why You Need This Book

♥

All this talk of building relationships and EntrepreFriendships may have you wondering how to actually go about doing this without seeming fake or creepy. You may be wondering how to make new connections with people you don't even know or how to take existing connections to the EntrepreFriendship level. You may be thinking all this EntrepreFriendship business sounds great, but you don't know a lot of people and don't know where to go to meet the right kind of people. Or you may be thinking, "I've been to the networking events and I'm online connecting with people, but I just don't feel like the right types of connections are out there for me." And you're wondering where the people you want to connect with are—you know, the ones who don't stare at you with a blank face or who gather in a corner with their friends and somehow didn't get the memo that they were at a networking event.

Networking events are for connecting and engaging with new people, not just hanging out with your familiar clique! If you're going to do that, just go somewhere else and save us all the uncomfortable, yet familiar, high-school feeling of lunchtime and the "popular table."

I sat with all sorts of people in high school—never the same folks every day. I guess I knew at an early age that increasing and diversifying your network always works out for a more well-rounded community and growth strategy. I was friends with everyone, and I take that same approach to building business relationships. (I was the homecoming queen for this precise reason, I think. I hope.) And I want to show you how to do the same (how to build relationships and EntrepreFriendships, not how to become homecoming queen; that ship has sailed).

What About the Introverts and Quiet Types?

♥

You may be the quiet type (not the bold, sassy woman with a real love for shiny and sparkly things) and like to stay to yourself, so the idea of reaching out to people seems frightening. I get it. Well, not exactly, as I'm not an introvert—but I understand what fear feels like. I understand what fear of failure, rejection, and embarrassment feels like. And I know what the temptation to succumb to those fears tastes like. I'm here to help you avoid that temptation and overcome that fear with confidence. I'm here to give you a tool that will help you understand how to navigate the otherwise-intimidating and overwhelming process of relationship building.

With this tool and faith, you'll likely have a lot more confidence in your ability to put yourself out there and build the relationships you really want to have. I can only imagine how being introverted and quiet can make building relationships 100 times more challenging, so I wrote this book to help relieve some of the tension and to help you take one step at a time to build real relationships.

In fact, the process is broken up into steps, because it's intended for you to take it one small step at a time. To do it any other way, especially for my beloved introverts and quiet types, is just too overwhelming. And remember: If you want to feel a little more comfortable, then consider going to the event with someone you trust, but avoid only engaging in conversation with that person. And be good to yourself after the event. Give yourself a positive pep talk and congratulate yourself for stepping outside of your comfort zone. This book will give you tools and strategies to build relationships that don't force you to be creepy or fake. It will also give you some steps and real suggestions/examples for filling in the unknowns that are often the reasons why you don't feel comfortable reaching out to people.

What if You're Already Really Busy?

♥

I know you're tempted to say you don't have time to put one more thing on your plate. Whatever you're doing in your business has to work toward a goal, an overall vision. So what are you doing in your business to build relationships, especially knowing the implications they can have on your business?

If you're not doing anything—or you're not doing anything strategically—then it's time to take a long, hard look at your schedule to determine what's priority, what's busywork, and what can be outsourced so you can take some time to devote to building relationships, especially EntrepreFriendships.

That's why I wrote this book for you: to give you a tool that would not only tell you how important it is to have business relationships and EntrepreFriendships and why you need them, but also to show you how to create and build them, even around your busy schedule.

By breaking up the process into steps, you are able to move at your own pace, but commit to working on the process on a steady and continual basis, especially once you get to Step 5, with a strategy you can incorporate to create and nurture EntrepreFriendships into your schedule, and make it a part of your regular, day-to-day business routine.

What if I Get Rejected?
I Hate Rejection!

♥

Me, too. No one wakes up and says, "I want to get rejected today" or "I want to get my feelings hurt and feel like no one really likes me"! No one says that, and if they do, then—well, I don't know. But I can tell you that rejection is a part of the process.

Changing dirty diapers is a part of the process of taking care of babies, yet many men and women willingly welcome new babies into their families every single day. They know that changing diapers is a part of the process, but that part of the process is small and insignificant compared with the joy and pleasure of having a family to love and nurture. Yes, it's challenging at times, but it's also very fulfilling. The same is true with building relationships: It's challenging at times, but also very fulfilling. So if you avoid them at risk of being rejected, then you'll never experience the fulfillment and the fruitfulness of having meaningful business relationships.

The rejection will come in all sorts of ways. It's best that I be real and up-front about this with you now. I don't want you to think that everyone you want to build a business relationship with will want to build one with you, even if you follow these steps. Not every email will get a reply, and not every phone call will be returned, or even answered. And not every invite will be accepted. It's just the way it is, and it can sting, but it's a part of the process. I am a super-sensitive person and it still hurts my feelings sometimes when the rejections come, especially from people I've built a relationship with, but then I'm reminded to activate my self-pity evacuation plan. I try to avoid taking myself down the slippery slope of beating up myself and feeling even worse, because that only makes the rejection go even deeper. Then, if you're not careful, you'll find yourself avoiding situations that may result in rejection—and that's when you lose out on opportunities.

So, activate the self-pity evacuation plan by doing one or all of the following:
- Take care of yourself.
- Talk it out with someone you know and trust.
- Remind yourself of things you like about yourself.
- Remind yourself that you're not for everyone and not everyone is for you.
- Remind yourself that you're closer to great opportunities.

Why I Wrote This Book for You

♥

I love when a complicated or unfamiliar task is broken down into steps that I can take one at a time. That's one of the easiest and best ways to accomplish a big goal or task. I know that building relationships that are meaningful and serve everyone well can seem like a big goal, with no clear steps about how to get there. This book gives you the steps. This step-by-step guide breaks down the otherwise-unfamiliar and overwhelming process of creating and nurturing business relationships and EntrepreFriendships into manageable and actionable pieces. The methods here are tried and true, and I can tell you they work.

I originally created this guide for my one-on-one clients and soon discovered, after using it for a team training with one of my clients, that it needed to be a resource for everyone. I didn't want to only make it available for my private clients. Rather, I wanted more people to know and understand how to go about building real business relationships. I wanted to show people how simple it is to build relationships when you have the right mindset and the right tools.

You don't have to be fake or creepy; you just need to know what to do. I truly believe that many entrepreneurs approach networking without a strategy or any clear idea of how to make the best of it, which leads to a room full of people who are uncomfortable, disengaged, and ineffective in building real business relationships. Yet, they'll show up next month, same time and same place, hoping the next time will be different—only perpetuating this vicious cycle of ineffective and uncomfortable networking that hardly leads to anything substantial.

Instead, only the extroverts and the ones who are really great at meeting and connecting with people seem to win: the natural great connectors who really don't put much thought or effort into it, because they're just really great with people naturally. You quietly love and envy them—but you don't have to, because this book will show you how to do what they seem to do so effortlessly, but instead with a step-by-step strategy.

The Mindset of "Support and Serve"

♥

Everyone starts somewhere. You've heard that saying before and you know it in your heart, but somehow you attempt to convince yourself that you're supposed to start at the top. You've convinced yourself, by comparing who you are to people next to you or the ones ahead of you, that you're supposed to have what they have, without realizing they didn't start there (at their desired level of success). No one starts there and no one gets there all alone. Yes, there are those who lie, cheat, steal, and abuse their way there, but if you're reading this book I'm willing to bet those pink pumps again that you're not trying to get there by doing that. You want to feel good about the legacy you build and the impact you have in others' lives. So you want to achieve your desired level of success (that is, get there) in a way that you'll be proud of. I'll show you the way to approach this. It's really simple.

It starts with this: **Adapt a mindset and heart for supporting and serving others.** I know that sounds simple and perhaps a little sappy, and maybe it is, but it still remains true. Those who support and serve others are the ones who get there in a way they can feel proud of. They are the ones who make the most impact on others and have the most meaningful relationships. To give you an example, allow me to introduce you to someone who is the ultimate example of support and service. That's Jesus Christ. It doesn't matter if you believe in Him as your savior or as a man that walked on this earth for 30-plus years; the reality is He supported and served others His entire life and left a lasting impact on the lives of generations to come. Even if you don't believe in Christianity, you can't deny that there's been no other living being who's ever been able to leave such a lasting and powerful impact on humanity. (The book *Marketing Like Jesus* by Darrin Shearer does an excellent job of breaking down the incredibly effective strategies that Jesus used to spread His message and leave His living legacy.)

If you want to make an impact on others and leave a powerful and inspiring legacy, then adapting the mindset of "support and serve" will allow you help more people while you grow your business. The mindset of "support and serve" is helpful to others and to you, because it removes the expectation of "I'm not doing this or that unless I'm getting something out of it" and replaces that with "Supporting and serving others is my 'getting something out of it.'"

And I know this can go against popular business messages about growing your business and profitability, but you gain more than just a great feeling when you support and serve others. You also gain opportunities to share your brand and connect it with others. So, let's be crystal clear: You can't take "support and serve" to the bank and deposit it in your banking account, but you can create opportunities that can turn into revenue streams by supporting and serving others. Think about it. Your chances of building a relationship with someone you don't know by supporting and serving them in a helpful way are far greater than showing up and asking them to do things for you, or expecting them to buy from you, just because you say they should.

The mindset of "support and serve" will truly change the way you look at your business opportunities and your business relationships. And here's a bit of a pro tip when it comes to this mindset: It can certainly help your business grow when clients are trying to decide who to hire. When they feel like you're in it for them and not just for the money, this can certainly work in your favor. But be careful to not allow people to take advantage of this. It's important to maintain control over your choices and create boundaries so lines are not crossed and your talent and time remain honored and valued.

Check Your Motives

♥

The steps in this book work. They help you get noticed, build connections, and build your brand. They are the steps to take to go from not having many business connections to having plenty of the right business connections. I believe in the steps in this book. But I have to caution you about your motives. If you approach these steps with only the intention of you getting something out of it, then you'll find yourself feeling unfilled and icky inside. It's a thin line, because in this book I show you the benefits of building business relationships and how they can positively affect your business, so it's easy for the motive to be making it only about you.

But, be careful, my friends, because when it's only about you and what you can get out of it, then you just may find much more resistance. So just be mindful of your motives before proceeding with building a business relationship. If you keep a heart of support and serve, you'll be great shape.

A Little About Me

♥

What's the one thing that excites you the most about life?
For me, it's striving to live a life full of passion and purpose with a steadfast commitment to glorifying God. I know part of my purpose is to shine bright, not so you see me, but so that you see God. My purpose allows me to turn up your bright so you can shine brighter in business in and in life. This business is my ministry, because I know you're most fulfilled and connected with God, with yourself, and with others when you do what you are called to do, which helps you grow in business and in life.

Who am I?
To know me is to know that I am creative, insightful, and incredibly compassionate. One of my natural gifts is the ability to create a safe place for you to be just who you are, while encouraging you to be your best authentic self. I'm an award-winning creative artist, a strategic thinker, a natural big-bold dreamer, and an exceptional strategist, mentor, author, and speaker. I am a deeply rooted woman of faith, a passionately committed wife and mother, and a dedicated, spirit-filled entrepreneur with a humble abundance of knowledge and experience.

My "why"
I do everything in my business to help restore hope within you and in your business so you can shine brighter in business and in life, because I believe we all have a purpose and a light within us that's

destined to shine bright. When we feel like we're ▮, overwhelmed, and not shining bright, it's easy to fe▮ up—to lose hope. I've been there. I know what it's like t▮ giving up on yourself and to lose nearly all hope. And it was m▮ in God, support from others, and embracing that light that resto▮ that hope for me.

I am certain that my pain has become my passion that fuels my purpose: to create a safe place for you to be exactly who you are while encouraging you to be your best in business and in life. I am committed to supporting you to shine brighter by helping to restore that hope, to re-energize you, and to help you regain focus. The outcome is that you feel more connected to your purpose, and get more motivated and intentional about making the difference you were born to make while also shining brighter in business and in life.

Therefore, as a brand strategist and mentor, I will listen to what you want to accomplish and then work with you to create clear strategies and plans to achieve it. I work with you, because I believe we shine brighter together.

I know you want to grow as an entrepreneur and expand your business to make an undeniable difference in the lives of your clients and in the community, so it starts with you. That's why I'm here: I'm here for you. I want to see you win. When you win, we win; and when we are winning, we can change the world. Together we can change lives and make a real difference.

What I do, and who I work with
Simply said, I bring out the best in you and turn up your bright. I support you in a few different methods, such as one-one-one support, personal and business training/workshops, books/resources, and public speaking. I focus on supporting you in areas that affect your ability to grow in business and in life.

I work primarily with entrepreneurs that advise and educate their clients in the finance and insurance industry. Many of my clients

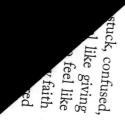

t, but know there's more, something bigger, ...ire how to get there. Oftentimes, my clients ...n business for five years or more, work full- ...and have a desire to feel more fulfilled, feel ...re money, and make a greater impact. They're ...nd are very devoted to their vision.

...ehensive inside-out approach to personal and business growth and development. My goal is to help my clients embrace authenticity and achieve their definition of success.

I offer complimentary strategy sessions, and more info about my services can be found on my website (www.MoniqueMelton.com).

Where it all began

I was the little girl who could be friends with anyone and even the one that stood up to the bullies. I was the girl voted "Most Friendly" in school, because I strive to make people feel comfortable with being just who they are, right in their moment. I was the homecoming queen in high school, because I could hang out and get along with anyone. I was the college student whom everyone on my dorm room floor wanted to talk to about life, because I really listened and cared. I remember and know exactly what it feels like to feel insecure about yourself and unsure if anyone even cares. So, I strive to create that safe place for people to be exactly who they are while encouraging them to be their best authentic self.

I absolutely love connecting with people by seeing the good in them and bringing out the best in them. I have a God-given gift for creating a safe and comfortable place for people to be their real, unedited selves, while inspiring them to be better and better. I have gathered from experience, education, and training how to connect and relate to people. And as a creative brand strategist and mentor, I understand just how to support women to shine brighter in business and in life.

I have a BA in social science with an emphasis in sociology and psychology and two years of graduate education in clinical counseling from Johns Hopkins. I combine 10 years of experience of being an entrepreneur in the wedding/beauty/retail industry with my education and real-world experience to provide comprehensive brand development for my clients. From defining who you are as an entrepreneur, to developing the foundation of the brand to creating systems and structure, to developing new products and services and an incredible client experience, I focus on building a dynamic brand. Visit my website (www.MoniqueMelton.com) to learn more about my journey.

It's more than the bottom line

It's about feeling a connection in your life, in your craft, and in your community. The bottom line is important, yes. And you need real results so your business can grow and thrive.

May the bottom line not be the only focus of why you do what you do, as this can lead to burnout, confusion, disappointment, and a lack of fulfillment. I believe that when you have a core connection with God, when you love what you do, and when you do it with passion and purpose, then you can truly embrace and enjoy the fruits of your labor, as they will come in many forms.

My BIG vision

Every passionate woman will have the confidence to embrace authenticity and achieve her definition of success.

What motivates me

I am an intentionally loving wife and mother; my family gives me so much motivation to be better than my best. My spiritual relationship with God, my love and desire to be more like Jesus Christ, and my devotion to serving people with genuine compassion, love, commitment, and integrity define my position in this industry and allow me to pursue each task with sincere enthusiasm, passion, and dedication.

My core values

1. Speak life.
2. Build real relationships.
3. Communicate openly and honestly.
4. Support and serve others.
5. Embrace authenticity.
6. Intentionally create value.
7. Problems have a solution. Find it, be it, or create it.
8. Have more integrity and humility than pride.

We shine brighter together

Give me gold, sequins, stripes, and bows, and you'll have one happy-sassy soul sister. To know me is to also know I love to shine and sparkle, inside and out. So I love a sparkly shirt or accessory and pretty pumps. I've even been told, "You sparkle everywhere you go." I love to shine bright, so you can shine brighter. I truly believe we shine brighter together!

So, when you work with me, you can expect to experience a refinery process that will push you out of your comfort zone, so you can continually be better than your best in business and in life.

Anything worth cherishing goes through a process, a necessary phase of development to ensure that all that is meant to be will be. You are worth it. Your purpose is worth it.

Because of my God-given gift for creating a safe place and my commitment to supporting my clients to shine brighter in business and in life, my clients see clear and substantial personal and business growth as a result of working together. I have a process that requires my clients to be real, honest, and true about who they are and what they really want to accomplish. Thus we can work together to develop plans and strategies to get there, but they have to do the work. I can't do the work for them. Because my clients are willing to do the work, then they are reaping the benefits. And while everyone's results will vary, I have yet to work with a client that hasn't experienced some level of personal and/or business growth. I believe in my process and I am grateful to share it with genuine honesty, support, and creativity.

And because I know how powerful business relationships and EntrepreFriendships can be in brand growth and development, they're the central focus of the marketing strategies I develop with my clients. Thus, this book had to be available to everyone. I had to share something with you that I believe will truly change the way you see your business relationships and the impact you and others can really have on your community.

This book will get you thinking, and if you're serious it will get you doing things that are unconventional—not because they're revolutionary, but instead because they go back to the roots and the basics of humanity.

Somehow in our over-connected, yet disconnected, world, we've lost touch with the ability to be in real relationships. So this book brings it back to the good stuff—the stuff we were made to have in our lives: real relationships. So come along with me as I show you, step by step, how to create and build business relationships and EntrepreFriendships.

And as you build your EntrepreFriendships I want to hear from you. I want you to share on social media with @moemotivate using the hashtag #EntrepreFriendships.

How This Book Works

♥

In this guide I'll show you the step-by-step process of finding and building business relationships and EntrepreFriendships. I'll share the steps and prompt you to take action, because knowing the process is part one, but taking action and doing the work (part two) are what really moves you forward. And part three is the part we all want, but in order to get there you have do parts one and two. Part three is reaping the rewards of having great business relationships and EntrepreFriendships; it's the bonds that are made, the opportunities that are created, the networks and communities that are grown and supported, and the countless ways of being advocates, supporters, and encouragers of others in business. Doesn't part three sound awesome?

If you think so, then continue reading this step-by-step process to building business relationships. You will want to keep this guide in your office and with you everywhere you go, because it will give you the tools you need to make the most out your business relationships and EntrepreFriendships. And if you care about your business relationships and EntrepreFriendships (or the potential ones), then this is a book you want to recommend others read as well. The more people who know and understand how to build supportive and mutually beneficial business relationships, the greater the impact we all can make.

Also, it's important for you to remember that the step-by-step process doesn't have to be fully linear; as you evolve and grow you may want to adjust your approach. And as you read this book, it's okay to not have all of the answers. It's okay to give yourself some time to explore, think, and really dig deep. Don't rush this process. Building business relationships is one of the most important things you can do for your business, and it starts with you. So give yourself time to grow and develop. You'll see more about what I mean when you review the activities in the Appendix, and you can also learn more about self-discovery by reading my book *Threads Unraveled*. *Threads Unraveled* encourages you to embrace who you are, what you want, and the purpose for your life.

How to Make the Most of This Book

♥

I created a companion relationship-building chart to go along with this book. You can access it by visiting my website (www.MoniqueMelton.com). The chart is a place for you to organize the information you gather as you build your strategy to connect and build relationships. You'll have a place to list the events, keep track of the connections you want to make, and track the connections you're making, plus much more. As you go through this guidebook, you'll want to fill in the details and necessary information in that chart.

(Note: You can work on the information in this book without this chart. The chart simply provides a central and organized location to keep track of the relationships you're building and the ones you desire to build.)

Tip: To get the most out of this book, read through this book once as if it were a textbook. Then re-read it, reading it like a workbook the second time, and going through the steps and phases as you read. Remember that each step takes time and results are gradual.

What This Book Is Not

♥

This is not a book to explore theory and the complexities of psychology, human growth and development, relationships, and sociology. This is a living guidebook designed to give you real-life steps toward building business relationships. This book is focused primarily on building in-person connections, but the following section is dedicated to building relationships online.

We are such an online–virtually connected world that I would be remiss to exclude online relationship building, but because nothing can replace in-person connections, the focus remains on those. This book is not designed to give medical, mental, spiritual, or any legal advice.

Building Relationships with Social Media

Though the primary focus of this book is on building relationships via in-person connections and opportunities, I want to give you a few strategies for building relationships and earning opportunities to grow in business with social media. I'm not a social media expert or strategist, but I do know quite a bit about building relationships, so the principle of support and serve remains at the heart of all of these strategies. While these strategies can work on most social media networks, they are particularly helpful in social media groups, such as Facebook groups. Those strategies are as follows:

Introduce yourself with a photo

You may know that it's important to introduce yourself online, especially when you're new to a group. And you might be thinking, "My photo is my profile picture. Isn't that enough?" No. You want it to stand out and be seen so people will recognize and remember you. You can also post pictures with other posts to have the same effect.

Connect with the group host and ambassadors

The host of the group and the ambassadors/moderators of the group are likely respected by the members. Making a connection with them would be a great way to gain favor in the eyes of the other members. You can connect with the host in the same ways mentioned throughout this book. Remember to stay genuine and look for ways to support and serve.

Connect with frequent posters

The frequent posters (not the spammers or the ones who only post looking for business) are likely interested in building relationships and connecting in the community, so they may be good people to get to know. If they post frequently and people engage in their posts, then they may also be respected by the members, which would make them good connections to make.

Write posts that invite conversation and engagement

If you want to build relationships online, you have to create conversations and engage in conversations. Thus, posting comments that invite conversation by asking for feedback, opinions, thoughts, or advice is a great way to spark conversation. Be mindful of the group rules and avoid sounding like you're trying to sell people on something. Most groups have a place where you can promote your business to get business, so make use of those and avoid doing direct promoting outside of that, unless the information is solicited.

Engage with other posts

Just as you want people to engage on your post, so do the other members in the group. I like to find posts that don't have any comments or only have a few, because I feel like I can be more helpful, rather than contributing to a post with several comments. When people post in groups, they are often looking for help in some way, so offering help to someone who otherwise has not been noticed by the other members is very rewarding. Posting in a group, large or small, can feel intimating, because you run the risk of being rejected, ignored, or not accepted. So engage and respond to posts as often as you can. Also, if you don't have the answer the person is looking for, you can still respond with words of encouragement. For example, if someone posts they are looking for referrals for a health coach, but I didn't have anyone to refer, I could still engage in the post by saying, "I don't know anyone, but I wish you success in your journey of working with a health coach. Here's to great health!"

Follow up offline (schedule an in-person or virtual meeting)

This one is simple, but it is often overlooked. Making connections online, via email, and in groups is great, but having a one-on-one phone call or meeting can be even more in-depth and beneficial for both parties. Also, when you've connected with someone online by being helpful, consider sending an email to follow up on the information you helped them with.

Volunteer to meet a need for the group

This goes back to the principle of support and serve. Contact the host to find out specific ways you can support the group.

Attend live events, if possible

The personal connection is unmatched. Live events hosted by people you've met online, especially those who host online groups, are great ways to deepen the connection and build support. Use the strategies shared in this book while at live, in-person events.

Use groups to conduct market research

You can use the group for research by posting direct research questions or by studying the questions and comments shared by others as they relate to your business.

Refer other people

I'm not active in a lot of groups, because I don't have the time to commit to them. Something I notice that really shows your commitment to serving and supporting others, and is thoroughly effective in gaining a favorable view from the members in the group, is to refer others. When you refer someone you not only help the person whom you referred, but you've also helped to solve a problem for the person looking for the referral, and you've added value to the community by keeping it a place where people can be supported, and you've helped yourself seem more supportive of others.

Share your wins

Many people like to see others succeed, especially because it shows them that it's possible for their business, too. Not everyone shares this same feeling when they see others succeeding, because they may be struggling with insecurities and jealously, but you can't let this keep you from celebrating your success. Sharing your wins is a great way to highlight your business and to showcase the value you're capable of delivering to your clients.

Step 1: Assess Your Business Relationship–Building Skills

Before you start networking and building relationships it's important to assess your skills and decide on a strategy. In order to get better at networking, you first need to discover where you are with your networking skills, and then build upon that. Step 1 will give you an idea of where you are now (and the following steps will show you how to build a networking strategy). Also, review the questions provided in the Appendix to help you explore this further. These questions will provide an introduction to self-discovery. (More is shared in my book *Threads Unraveled*, which is helpful for improving your business relationship–building skills.) It's important to understand that the essence of building business relationships, as well as personal relationships, is to support and serve others. At the core of it all is the ability to connect with people by supporting and serving them. That means helping them grow and being of service to them in some way, even if it's small. So remember, as you embark on this journey: Keep your eyes on ways to support and serve others, and you'll go much further. Answer the following questions to make an assessment:

1. What type of networking events do you already attend? (A healthy number is one to two events per week.)

2. What type of online business groups are you in? (A healthy number is active participation in one to three groups.)

3. What type of networking events do you like to attend and why? (Strive for a nice variety of mixers, workshops, traditional networking events, and others.)

4. What is your follow-up strategy for networking or when you meet new people?

5. How often do you stay connected with people you meet at networking events or online?

• How can you improve this?

6. How much time do you spend preparing to engage at a networking event?

7. Think about how you present yourself at networking events or online. What are three things that you do really well, and what are three areas that you can improve?

8. What do you want people to remember about you the most when you go to a networking event or engage online?

• How can you make this clear?

9. What do you want people to remember the most about your services and your company?

• How can you make this clear?

10. What is the most interesting aspect you can share about your business?

11. What are some of the pain points of the audience attending the event or participating in the online community?

  • What are some of their needs/wants/problems as they relate to business and/or their personal lives?

  • How can you make a connection with them on one or more of these issues?

12. How do you introduce yourself?

  • Have you included what you do, whom you do it for, why you do it, and how you do it different than anyone else?

  • How can you communicate this effectively and concisely?

• Write what you do in 10–15 words or less.

13. Who's your ideal client/customer? (List here the top seven to 10 characteristics and descriptions that define your dream client/customer.)

Note: At networking events, sometimes people will ask you to tell them an ideal referral for you, or they may ask you the type of clients you work with. It is helpful to be able to clearly and specifically explain the type of clients you are working to attract in your business.

14. What are some recent business successes?

15. What type of information or news would you like to share? (Think of events or activities, promotions, or news that you want to share.)

Step 2: Develop a Strategy for Navigating Live, In-Person Events

♥

Remember: The goal of networking is to meet people and build relationships. The indirect result can be geared toward business, such as clients and sales, but the direct goal is to meet people and figure out how you can support and serve them. This is the foundation of business relationships and EntrepreFriendships, and nurturing those relationships.

Part 1: What to Do Before the Event

Do Your Research
Research the event

Determine who will be there and what they are coming to do (i.e, is this a casual event, a leads group, structured with agenda, a mixer?), and find out the following information:
- People who typically attend
- Number of people
- Agenda (Find out how the meeting is typically conducted. In other words, what is the order of events/what's to be expected?)
- Cost to attend (Will drinks and food be included or provided?)
- Frequency of meetings
- Dress code
- Time and location

Research the attendees, speakers, and host

If a list of attendees is provided, this is a great way to find out about the people planning to attend the event. If the list is not provided, you can contact the host and ask about the type of people who typically attend the event. You also want to research the host. Here are some things you want to know about the attendees, speakers, and host:

- What type of business owners/people will be attending the event?
- How long have they been in business?
- What is the nature of their business?
- What do people who attend the event expect to get out of it?
- What are some specific ways your product or service could improve their business/life?
- Do they have any recent accomplishments that they are celebrating?

How to find this information
- Search their websites.
- Review their different social media profiles and the people they follow.
- Do a simple internet search.

Tip: Avoid requesting to make personal connections prior to meeting them or prior to following Step 5. This can come off as creepy—and you want to avoid creepy.

Determine how you can showcase
Find out if you can provide a door prize or a giveaway, or if you can do a brief business spotlight or present on a topic that would benefit the group. Being a guest speaker at an event is a great way to gain exposure and increase brand awareness, which can also result in new clients/customers.

You can also consider sponsoring the event in exchange for an opportunity to showcase your services/products in a presentation.

Decide what to wear

Be sure to dress according to the dress code and according to your brand identity. Physical attire is very important with regard to the way people perceive you.

Arrive early

Arriving early can help you avoid the feeling of walking in a room full of people you don't know and feeling uncomfortable, because you're not quite sure who to talk to or where to go. If you arrive early, you can greet people as they arrive and help them feel more comfortable, too.

Be prepared to be approached

Bring your business cards and wear a name tag. Keep your business cards within reach so you can easily distribute them. Be sure to ask for others' business cards. Be sure to smile, and avoid sitting alone or off in corner or against the wall.

Be prepared to approach people

Most of the time there will be a combination of people approaching you and you approaching people. I know it can be uncomfortable, but the more prepared you are for this the better. Practice, breathing deeply and reminding yourself that you're at the event to build relationships with people there to do the same thing as you are; this will hopefully help you ease your nerves so you can relax and have a nice time.

Practice the Standard Introductions

Practice the 30-second elevator speech

Use this when you are introducing yourself to a group or a room full of people.

Write your 30-second speech here:

How to write it

Include who you are, what you do, and the value you deliver (i.e., what problem do you solve?), why you do what you do, and how you do it differently than anyone else.

Practice the brief one-on-one introduction

Use this when you are introducing yourself to people individually.

Hi, my name is_____. (Offer a compliment with a question.) So, what are you most excited about right now? Or what motivated you to come here today? (Then, tell them what you're excited about in your business. Make sure you include the what, the who, the why, and how you're different.) Continue with "Engage in meaningful conversation" (see Part 2).

Part 2: Engage During the Event

Have great body language
- Smile.
- Nod your head in agreement.
- Make eye contact.
- Avoid crossing your arms.
- Lean forward to suggest engagement.
- Avoid using your cell phone.

Make introductions

Introduce yourself to everyone, if it's a small group. If the group is large, make a point to introduce yourself to several of the people there. Remember: Fewer meaningful connections are better than many shallow connections. Use the standard brief introduction you prepared in Part 1. Avoid trying to sell yourself; instead focus on getting to know them and building a business relationship.

Engage in meaningful conversation

It's important to approach and introduce yourself to people. That's why practicing your introductions is so important: It will help you when you're feeling nervous or uncomfortable. When you go to events, it's tempting to just stand around feeling uncomfortable, so to help avoid this make it a point to approach people and introduce yourself, then engage in meaningful conversation.

Review your research
You want to know a little about the background about the host, speakers, and attendees.

Know who you are
One of the best ways to avoid superficial and surface conversations is to talk about the things that your business stands for—your core values. Your core values set the tone for how you'll grow your business, build your team, and treat your clients. It's important to know what they are and to keep them on your mind. If you need help deciding on the core values of your brand, review the Core Values Activity in the Appendix. Thus, to keep the conversation meaningful, keep your core values in the forefront of your mind, so when you communicate you can demonstrate them as much as possible. For example, if you value relationships you may want to mention this and display this by engaging in thoughtful dialogue with others.

Know your why
Always be sure there's a why behind what you do.

Tip: Why you work and why you do the work you do are not necessarily the same. Instead, why you do the work you do is often more connected to you purpose, your past experiences, and the people in whose lives you want to make a difference. (For more help with working on your why statement, consider exploring my book *Threads Unraveled*.)

Know your message
What is the one message you want to get across about your brand? (Make this clear and memorable.)

Know what you want

Have a clear idea of the specific things you are looking for and specifically how people can help you. (But remember to focus on building relationships and not closing the sale.)

Determine your "call to action"

What is the specific action for the event that you want to share with others? What do you want people to do? How can they connect with you?

Bring your stuff

Bring any event invites, company brochures, samples, flyers, etc. that share more about what you do or for any upcoming promotions or events.

Bring the charm

When you meet people, give them a compliment with a question. Here are a couple examples: Your hair looks great; who's your stylist? That presentation was amazing; where did you draw your inspiration from?

Bring great questions

Ask open-ended questions, and use "why" to go deeper.

Think of different questions, topics, and information you may want to share or learn more about from a different business. You might ask variations of these questions:
- What's going great in life right now?
- What have you been up to since the last time we met?
- If you could have a re-do for last week, what would you change?
- What are your favorite kinds of community events?

Try questions like this if the person is in business:
- What are you most excited about right now?
- What successes are you celebrating in your business?
- What's your favorite kind of client to work with?
- What are the questions about your business that people ask the most?

- What do you wish more people knew about you?
- What goals are you working on right now?
- What are you most passionate about in your business?
- Do you have any projects or events coming up that you could use some help getting the word out about?

Try questions like this if the person is not a business professional or if this is a more personal setting:
- What are you most excited about right now?
- What successes are you celebrating in your life?
- What are your hobbies?
- What do you wish more people knew about you?
- What goals are you working on right now?
- What are you most passionate about in your life?

Identify common areas of interest and explore further
Ask about their background, their family, where they are from, and how they got started in their business. What goals are they working on this week?

Be positive and cheerful. Even if a person is negative or complaining, shift the conversation to positive.

Ask helpful questions
If you're in a group that is more structured and everyone is engaged around the same topic, this will help you stand out. Helpful questions are questions that can benefit the group at large and create more room for exploration and clarity. Avoid personal questions, as these can be viewed as being inconsiderate of others. Reserve personal questions for a later time.

For example:
Let's consider that the conversation is about how to identify your target audience and the speaker is reviewing the different steps.

Good questions:
- In step one you suggested we understand who we are as a person and have a clear understanding of how to communicate our why. Can you share a couple questions that could help us figure this out?
- In what ways is having a clear understanding of our target audience beneficial for our businesses?
- For those of us that just started, where would you suggest we go to find market research?

Personal questions to avoid:
- I don't know if I really understand how to say my why. Can I share it with you and you help me figure it out?
- I'm in the retail business and my store is located near downtown. Can you tell me who would be my target audience?
- I'm just getting started and I really can't seem to find any clients. What specifically should I be doing to attract clients into my business?

Ask for follow-up
After you have genuinely engaged in conversation (see above) with someone, the next step is to ask to have a follow-up meeting, one-on-one. The dialogue for this can go something like this: "It has been so great talking with you. I'd love to get together over a cup of tea/coffee to learn more about your business and how I may be able to support you/send you referrals. Do you think we can set something up for next week? I'd love to hear more about (mention something specific from the conversation)."

It's important to suggest a time, as to avoid the "sure, let's get together sometime" response. Most people who say that don't really get together and probably never intended to; it just seemed like the right thing to say.

You don't have to schedule the meeting right there, but you can inform them that you'll give them a call/text or send an email to confirm a date and location.

Be active and create credibility
If the event is structured to allow open conversation and dialogue for everyone, one person at a time, then support the conversation. (If in a group that is more structured and everyone is engaged around the same topic, this will help you stand out.)

Tip: Take photos while you're there at the event. You can use these to post on social media later or while at the event.

Close out of conversations, politely
"It was so great talking to you, (name). I really enjoyed getting to know more about (something specific from the conversation). I'll send you an email/text/give you a call to set up our coffee/tea meeting. I'm really looking forward to it."

If you didn't schedule or suggest a one-on-one (and you do not plan to do so) you can close out of a conversation like this:
"It was so great talking to you, (name). I really enjoyed getting to know more about (something specific from the conversation). This is such a nice event to meet and connect with new people. I'm sure you'd like to meet and connect with more people, so I'll let you go. It was really great talking to you."

At every event you want to prepare for the event, have engaging conversation, ask for the one-on-one (not with everyone you meet; I make a goal of at least one), and close out of conversations politely.

Introduce yourself to the host(s) of the event
- Thank them for hosting the event.
- Compliment them on the event, with a question.
- Be sure to ask them questions about their business.
- Consider asking them about what motivated them to host the event. (Remember the host may be very busy, so don't expect to spend a lot of time talking during the event. In the "Thank the host/event organizer" section in Part 4, you'll see more about how to connect with the host.)
- Identify a way to be helpful.

- Ask if you can help with anything.
- If you see the host packing up or cleaning up, go help.
- Help the host carry supplies/belongings. (Be sure to ask for permission first. If they don't know you, this may be uncomfortable.)
- Offer to help with taking notes.

Introduce yourself to the speaker
- Thank them for speaking at the event.
- Compliment them on their presentation, with a question.
- Be sure to ask them questions about their business.
- Consider asking them about what motivated them to speak at the event.
- Identify a way to be helpful.
- Ask if you can help with anything.
- If you see the speaker with packing up or cleaning up, help.
- Help the speaker carry supplies/belongings. (Be sure to ask for permission first. If they don't know you, this may be uncomfortable.)

Part 3: Support and Serve

While you're engaging in conversation, it's a great idea to learn ways you can be of service to the other person. Ask questions to find out how you can support or be of service to them--how you can add value. Find out about what they are working on and how you can help them. It doesn't have to directly relate to your business, but instead you can offer suggestions, referrals, recommendations, and more. Think as if a friend needed help; you would be willing to make yourself available to support and serve—with no strings attached.

Ask questions like this:
- What projects are you working on?
- What type of help would make it easier for you?
- What obstacles are you facing in your business right now?
- What's the perfect referral for you right now?
- What's the perfect connection for you right now?

Part 4: Engage in the Follow-Up Process

Take a few notes
How many people appeared to be at the event?
What did you get out of the event?
How many new connections did you make?
Who do you plan to follow up with?

Write something down about the people you connected with that will help you remember them and your conversation.

Follow up, right away
Follow up with those you suggested having a one-on-one meeting. Make email, phone, or text contact within 12 to 24 hours of initial greeting.

> **Example email or guide for phone conversation:**
> Hi, (name).
> It was great meeting you on (date) at the (event name). I really enjoyed our conversation and learning more about (specific conversation topic). I'm so glad you're interested in having a one-on-one meeting so I can learn more about your business and how I can perhaps send you more referrals or support you in some way. We didn't have a chance to pick a time and location so I wanted to send you an email/give you a phone call to follow up on that. Are you available to meet at (central or popular location) on one of the following dates/times (include three options)? I'm really looking forward to connecting, and I hope you have a great day.

Post on social media and tag the event and any others you met at the event. Mention that the event was great and you're looking forward to the next one. If you took photos while there, upload those, too.

> Example:
> The #(event hashtag) or @(event name) was really great. Can't wait for the next one.

Follow up with people with whom you engaged in conversation with, but did not suggest a one-on-one. Simply thank them for the time and, if you later decided you want to have a one-on-one, suggest that in the email.

> **Example:**
> Hi, (name).
> It was great meeting you on (date) at the (event name). I really enjoyed our conversation and learning more about (specific conversation topic). I really would enjoy learning more about your business so I can perhaps send you some referrals or support you in some way. Would you be interested in getting together over a cup of coffee? Are you available to meet at (central or popular location) on one of the following dates/times (include three options)? I'm really looking forward to connecting and I hope you have a great day.

Thank the host/event organizer

Send an email or thank-you note to host/event organizer. If you had a chance to engage in meaningful conversation with the host, be sure to include how you enjoyed something specific about the conversation. Ask how can volunteer in the group (and follow through on this).

> **Example:**
> Hi, (name).
> It was great meeting you on (date) at the (event name). I really enjoyed the event. Thank you so much for hosting. I really would enjoy learning more about how I can volunteer. I know planning and hosting events can be a lot of work and I'd be happy to know how I can help. I'd be interested in greeting the guests or even cleaning up after the event. I'd also really like to learn more about your business and perhaps how I can refer business to you. Perhaps we could get together over a cup of coffee and discuss this in more detail. Are you available to meet at (central or popular location) on one of the following dates/times (include three options)? I'm really looking forward to connecting and I hope you have a great day.

Reach out to missed connections

Send an email to people with whom that you were not able to connect, but wanted to.

In the email, introduce yourself and mention that you were at the same networking event (provide the date) and you wanted to introduce yourself. Let them know you would like to learn more about their business and ask if they plan to be at the next event. Or, you can suggest a one-on-one meeting.

Remember: In order for networking to work effectively you need to first have the right perspective. In other words, show up to build relationships, support, and serve others. Do the research, engage in meaningful conversation, support and serve, and follow up. And remember that the strength is in the follow-up, which many fail to do consistently. Here's a pro tip: Send your follow-up email before you head to your next destination. That way you don't forget. Or, if you prefer to call, make a note in your calendar to call (list specific contact information) on a specific date/time. Also, to avoid losing cards, download a business card reader app.

A note about online connections: Building business relationships can take place online and in person. When you meet people online it's important to practice the same steps provided in this in this book. It's also important to avoid coming on too strong too fast. Avoid requesting to be connected with them on their personal accounts before you've made a connection. Some people may find this off-putting. Also, remember to show up to be supportive and helpful. Do not add people to your groups without their permission, do not add people to your email list without their permission, and avoid spamming them with your promotions. (And don't worry: A lot of us have made some of these mistakes, so don't be too hard on yourself if you have. Now you know, and when we know better, we can make better choices.) The goal is to treat online relationships with respect and dignity. Give them time to grow and develop just like an in-person relationship.

Step 3: How to Find the Places to Meet People and Build Relationships

♥

Now that you understand your current networking skills and have developed a strategy for networking, it's time to locate the networking opportunities. Opportunities to connect with new people are all around us, but sometimes it can seem like finding the right kind of networking community is more work than you anticipated. If you know where to look, then you'll find it a lot easier to locate groups that you can be a part of and contribute to. The focus of your networking is to find people with whom you can build business relationships and EntrepreFriendships. Not everyone you meet will want to build a business relationship with you or will be a great EntrepreFriend. Steps 4 and 5 will help you figure out how to understand the different people you meet and how to spot potential business relationships.

Tip: When looking for a group, avoid making these hasty assumptions:
    "This group isn't right for me."
    "I'm not getting anything out of this."
    "The people in this group don't know my industry."

Before you decide to commit to building relationships within a particular group or community, give yourself some time to identify different ways you can contribute to the group. And then, give yourself some time to get to know the people that created the group and the members of the group or community. If you join a group or community only for the sake of getting something out of it, it can be really easy to throw in the towel before you've really gathered enough insight about the group.

Building relationships takes time, and it also takes time to get to know people in a group. It takes time to feel like you're able to support and serve, and get something out of it, too. Just like you are new to the group, they are also new to you; you are trying to figure one another out and decide if you want to get to know one another further. As easy and natural as it can seem to make quick assumptions, avoid this by following this rule when joining new groups: When joining new groups, commit to attending and engaging in at least four consecutive meetings. Each time, identify a way you can contribute and do it. For online groups, give yourself four months of actively engaging in the group.

So where can you find these groups? Where are all of these potential EntrepreFriendships hiding? Well, they aren't hiding; you just have to know where to find them. Later in this step are some tips for finding them. Before I tell you about where to find them, though, I want to give you some tips on what you're looking for in networking groups and communities.

1. A place where you're embraced, accepted, and acknowledged
2. A place where you will meet people who do not look or act exactly like you (Diversity is key.)
3. A place where you can connect with people with whom you can potentially do business or who can refer business to you, and where you can do the same for them
4. A place where you can have your voice heard and can have input
5. A place where you can make a commitment to support and get involved in some way
6. A place where many of the people have similar (not necessarily the exact same) interests (business or personal)

7. A place that is growing, not necessarily in size, but in knowledge, connectedness, and personal and professional development

The goal is to find a group that you can support and in which you can also feel supported. You want to be involved in a community that encourages you and its members to grow and connect with others. It's important to note that you may want to avoid the following type of communities: communities that only care about certain people (and not all of the members), are closed-minded, are unwilling to accept feedback and ideas from the members of community, and are mainly self-serving.

Now that you have some criteria for the groups you're looking for, here are the different ways to find groups.

Tip: Use the Building Relationships chart (available on my website: www.MoniqueMelton.com) to organize the information you collect from the following sources.

1. **Search online:** Use search engines, Eventbrite, Eventful, YouTube, LinkedIn, Instagram, Periscope, Twitter, Facebook, Meetup.com, NetParty, and Craigslist. Also consider your local community website for event listings. Use terms relevant to your industry and geographical location, and use hashtags. You may want to type in "networking in (your city)" when searching online. You can be specific to your industry, too; try "networking for (your industry) in (your city)." On Facebook and Meetup.com, you can look for local events. And on Facebook, you can search for groups by typing in your industry name, city, or something related to business, such as entrepreneurship, networking, or business. You can also check out the Femmeboss + Solo Girl Squad community of women. Femmeboss serves as a platform for ambitious women to connect for both work and play through popup coworking events, friendship matchmaking mixers, webinars, and more. Femmeboss aims to make networking for women more about fostering connections and building support systems rather than simply exchanging business cards. Just always remember to use caution when attending unfamiliar

events and consider attending the event with someone you know and trust. If you get an uncomfortable feeling, trust it.

2. **Consider online social media groups:** Social media groups on sites such as Facebook can be a great place to meet and engage with a lot of new people. In Facebook groups, take note of the admins, facilitators, and active users. These are the people who are likely great connectors—and are also showing up because they are looking to grow their business and to connect with others. I'm very active in specific groups on Facebook, and it's for a couple reasons: The groups are diverse and reflect community, the leaders are real and they value real community, the community is active and supportive, and the community is an environment of connections and shared resources. You can share your business info, but the groups aren't flooded with spam and promos, which makes it an enjoyable experience for everyone.

When looking for groups, be sure to read the rules and engage accordingly. Remember: The more you show up to give and support, the more support you'll likely receive. I've worked with many new amazing clients just by engaging and supporting in these online communities. Don't underestimate of power of engaging in online communities. It's important to remember that engagement is key, though. Don't simply show up and post your business info or constantly ask questions about your business without giving back more and more. Instead, comment on others' post, answer questions, and participate in the daily or weekly discussion topics presented by the admins or that a group hosts. It may take up more of your time, but you can schedule time in your day to engage so you can do it consistently. If you're looking for some great groups you can start with my growing group (Entrepreneurs Shine Bright with Monique Melton), Savvy Business Owners, Blink Conference, Boss Moms, and so many more.

3. **Ask around:** Contact your local colleges, small business association, chamber of commerce, women's business

organizations, community library, Business Network International, Rotary Club, mastermind groups, and local religious organizations. These community organizations often host events, classes, and workshops, and invite outside speakers to teach/speak. Compile a list of those speakers, hosts, and attendees that relate to your industry.

4. **Search community events:** When searching community events make a list of people who sponsor and host the events. The people who typically host or sponsor events can make great business relationships, because they are typically well connected or are looking to make more connections. Either way, it's worth noting who they are so you can reach out. (I'll show you how to reach out to new people in Step 5.)

5. **Search content:** Look at local and international blogs, newspaper articles, and local magazines, and take note of the authors of those articles. The people who typically write and publish articles are likely to get increased feedback and brand awareness from their publications. They can make great business relationships, too, for the same reasons as community event hosts: They are typically well connected or are looking to make more connections. (Again, I'll show you how to reach out to new people in Step 5.)

6. **Connect with people:** Consider reaching out to lawyers, doctors, and professors and advisors at universities and colleges, as well as committee members of networking groups and associations, and bankers. All of these types of business professionals interact with different people all of the time, which means they are likely to be great connectors and resources for information about what's happening in the community and who to go to in the community for things you're looking for.

Take action: Research the events in your area. List networking events in your area you would be interested in attending on the accompanying Building Relationships chart.

Step 4: Understand the Different Types of People You Meet

♥

The business connections you make can potentially affect your business in different yet helpful ways. Many of the people you meet can be a potential benefit or asset to your business in one way or another, because each person can potentially have a different role in your business. Thus, it's helpful to understand the different categories/roles of people—and how each can affect your business.

Just as in our personal lives, in which we have different types of roles and relationships (such as mother, sister, friend, spouse, child, and so on), we also have different type of relationships in business. Those relationships and roles can be categorized into five key areas: influencers/connectors, connected to influencers, influencer supporters, colleagues, and good connections. Any of these relationships can progress to the EntrepreFriendship level. (In Step 6, I show you how to build the EntrepreFriendship.)

It's important to note that the goal is not to build EntrepreFriendships with everyone you meet or everyone on your list, because that would be nearly impossible to maintain. However, it is possible to have a variety of business relationships and several EntrepreFriendships.

In this step, I help you understand how to connect with and benefit from the different types of people you meet. You can also use this information to help you build a list of people you need to be connecting with in your business. As you go through the research process here, you can use the Building Relationship chart from my website (www.MoniqueMelton.com) to add the names of people you want to connect with and the people you've already connected with at some time. The more organized you can be and the more strategic you can be with finding future connections, the more effective you can be in building business relationships.

Tip: If you're the fancy type, make it a goal to build your list to 100 people that you would like to connect with at some time in the future. And use these words of wisdom to help you organize the people you meet and want to meet:

Don't begin aligning or teaming up (building a business relationship or EntrepreFriendship) with anyone without doing your research about them to be sure their core values, business ethics, and reputation support your brand.

To help you keep things organized, use the Building Relationships chart to keep up with the different people you meet and the EntrepreFriendship you want to build. If you want to be most effective and really prepared, and thus make the most out of your time and energy, work on the chart before engaging in the process of building business relationships and EntrepreFriendships. The goal is to do the research first and as you go along. After you've researched and met different people at networking events, you'll find that there are several people with whom you'd like to build an EntrepreFriendship. By completing the chart and doing the research on the potential EntrepreFriendships, your chances of smoothly and successfully navigating this process of building EntrepreFriendship is a lot more favorable.

A reminder about the Building Relationships chart: You can work on the information in this book without this chart. The chart simply provides a central and organized location to keep track of the relationships you're building and the ones you desire to build.

Categories Defined

Influencers and connectors

An influencer/connector is someone who has an established platform or community that trusts them, values their opinion, and will often follow their advice. They have people who listen to them simply because it's coming from them, and they are often very connected. Because they know so many people, they are often really great at connecting with people.

How influencers/connectors help your business: Having relationships with influencers/connectors is one of the best ways to accomplish increasing your brand awareness and getting your name and brand out there to as many new people as possible, but in a very genuine and trustworthy way. An influencer/connector can have an active and supportive community of 10K people. By being referred or supported by this influencer/connector, you can reach that audience much faster and easier than trying to reach each person individually. This saves you time and money. Also, when you offer support and show love to an influencer/connector it is often noted and remembered. As influencers/connectors grow in popularity and reach larger audiences, so do the number of people who reach out to them asking and requesting something. So when someone shows up without an agenda to get something from them, but to instead do something for them, it gets noticed. I share how to support influencers in Step 5.

Connected to influencers/connectors

This is like the influencer's/connector's bestie. This person is close and well connected to the influencer/connector. They are often seen with the influencer/connector, and the influencer/connector will often refer to or recommend this person. They may not necessarily have a large platform or community of their own, but they are often well received by the influencer's/connector's community and highly trusted.

How connected to influencers /connectors help your business: If you want to get to an influencer/connector, sometimes the best way to go about it is to build a relationship with the connected one. Get to know this person and develop a real bond, while also finding out ways you can support and serve the influencer/connector. Connected to influencers/connectors can also help you gain some notoriety within a community, which works to help you build trust and likability with a community that you really want to serve.

Influencer/connector supporters

An influencer/connector supporter is often seen celebrating, sharing, and advocating for influencers/connectors, with or without acknowledgment of the influencer/connector. This person can also be considered as a brand ambassador, someone who will support and endorse your brand because they have benefited from it and believe in what your brand is all about. This person is motivated by their personal experience or encounter with the brand or the influencer and finds it rewarding to help support the influencer—without any strings attached.

How influencer/connector supporters help your business: This is very similar to connected to influencers/connectors. One thing to add is that collaborating with supporters and bringing your energy together can help you have a great impact in the community, get noticed by the influencers/connectors and the community, and create new opportunities.

Industry colleagues

Some may refer to this as your competition, but industry colleagues are your fellow business connections. They may or may not be in your industry, and you're often on the same playing field.

How industry colleagues help your business: You can be great accountability partners, and you can learn and support one another as you grow. Even your competitors can make great connections to have, even if for nothing less than to keep you providing better services and products for your community and clients.

Good connections

A good connection is someone who may or may not be in your industry or affiliated with a particular business, but who is well connected. They have inside access to people you want to meet and build relationships with, or they know how to connect you to people. They are often very resourceful and can usually have the connection for you—or will find out where to get it for you.

How good connections support your business: A good connection is as simple as it sounds. They can help you reach and connect with people you otherwise wouldn't have been able to reach. They can make an introduction, which can make the connection a lot smoother.

Words of wisdom: It's important to have a nice mixture of business relationships and EntrepreFriendships, so avoid loading yourself with only one type of business relationship. You want to get out there and have diversity in the relationships you have with others. Also, you can be considered one or all of these different types of roles to different people, so don't underestimate the value you bring to the relationship.

A note about influencers/connectors: Connecting with people who are connected with the influencers/connectors is often step one to reaching the influencers/connectors. Connecting with people who are supporters of the influencers/connectors is another step to gaining the attention of the influencers/connectors.

Key Characteristics of the Different Roles
(Ideally, they should meet all of these, but at least most is good.)

Characteristics of influencers/connectors:
- Their values align with yours; they have a similar mission.
- You are excited about what they are doing in the community.
- You want to see their mission succeed.
- You have some key common interests.
- They influence your target audience.
- They have a large community influence.

- They have a large following of engaged followers.
- They are well known in their industry.
- You genuinely honor and value them as a person.

Characteristics of connected to influencers/connectors:
- They endorse the influencer.
- They are an affiliate of the influencer.
- The influencer mentions them.
- The influencer showcases or spotlights their work.

Characteristics of influencer supporters:
- They endorse the influencer, with or without recognition.
- They comment, share, and talk about the influencer often.
- They put into practice things that the influencer shares/teaches.

Characteristics of industry colleagues:
- They may be in your industry.
- They work with your target audience or those connected to your target audience.

Characteristics of good connections:
- They can have any or all of the qualities listed above.
- They may not be in business, but may be well connected.

Characteristics of an Ent勞epreFriendship

Any of the roles listed in this step can make for a great EntrepreFriendship. When looking for an EntrepreFriendship you also want to look for someone with the following characteristics:
- They are active in the community (online or offline).
- They are friendly and supportive of others.
- They are devoted to building a great brand.
- They are connected with others or have a desire to do so.
- You see this person often (online or offline).
- They have a positive reputation.
- They are building a brand with integrity.

Note: Handle with care or avoid people who are very negative and who rarely support others.

Step 5: Get Noticed and Connect with Influencers/Connectors

❤

Building connections and creating EntrepreFriendships with influencers/connectors is a key and necessary ingredient in building brand awareness, diversifying your community, accessing new opportunities, and building relationships with more people. This step shows you how to build relationships with influencers/connectors. You can also use the process to connect with any of the different roles from Step 4, even if they have a very large platform and do not know you at all. Remember: Industry influencers/connectors can also become EntrepreFriends.

Part 1: How to Spot a Great Influencer/Connector

Identify people in your industry or affiliated industry (they may or may not be in your industry) and find those who:

1. Are writing about topics related to your industry on blogs, and in magazines and publications.

2. Are speaking and teaching at workshops and conferences.

3. Are featured on Periscope interviews, Blab, blog articles, podcast, YouTube, TV shows, radio stations, newspapers, magazine, and social media and other channels that promote different industry leaders.

4. Are authors in your industry or of interest to your target audience.

5. Have programs, courses, workshops, and books, or teach on topics in your industry.

6. Are well connected with the people with whom you desire to build connections.

7. Host events/networking opportunities.

8. Are members of community organizations, such as your local chamber of commerce.
- Look for those who are on committees.
- Look for those who are on the board.
- Look for those who are active and involved.

Part 2: Invest in Them

What type of products or services do they have that you can genuinely support?

1. Invest in it, and share about your experience with it. (Share with your networks, your friends, online, and on social media.)

2. Take a picture of you enjoying it or the impact it's made on your life, and tag them in a social media post.

3. Send them a personalized thank-you letter.
- Start with what you invested in.
- Share how it improved your life in some way.
- Share why you believe others should use it.
- Share how you have told others about it and ask how you can help support them further.

Part 3: Support and Serve

Look for ways you can support what they're doing.

1. Share their social media post.

2. Volunteer at their events.

3. Participate on committees.

4. Send them positive words of encouragement.

Part 4: Connect with Them on Social Media/Blogs

1. Follow their blog and comment on posts frequently. You can subscribe to their site to stay updated. Make helpful comments and engage with other commenters.

2. Engage with them on social media.
- Share their content.
- Retweet their info.

- Comment on their posts.
- Use their hashtags to continue the conversation.
- Curate their content and share on your page.
- Subscribe to their mailing list and invite others to do the same.

Part 5: Directly Connect with the Influencer/Connector

Make connection via email or phone.

1. Greet with a compliment.
2. Personalize the email.
   - Mention where you met, if you've met. If not, mention how you came across their work or their business. (Perhaps you saw their post in an online group, or someone shared their website. List the specific way you found them.)
   - Tell them how much you value (specifically) what they are doing and how it relates to your personal mission.
   - Continue with what you invested in.
     - Share how it improved your life in some way.
     - Share why you believe others should use it.
     - Share how you have told others about it and ask how you can help support them further.
   - Share your mission (briefly).
   - Share how you would love to support them (specifically). Choose one of the following:
     - Referrals
     - Attend their event
     - Spread the word
   - Ask how you can support them.
3. In the reply email, offer to have a one-on-one to discuss how you can give them referrals.
   - You can do this in person or online. I show you how to have a one-on-one in Step 6.

It's important to note that connecting with influencers/connecters may not always work out in your favor. Once you've met several people and have built your list of people you'd like to meet and people you've already met, it's important to figure out with whom you want to build EntrepreFriendships.

Step 6: Build the EntrepreFriendship

♥

The previous steps showed you how to build a networking strategy and build business relationships. Step 6 helps you determine how to turn business relationships into EntrepreFriendships. Remember: The difference between a great business relationship and an EntrepreFriendship is that an EntrepreFriendship is more involved and intentional. The relationship is more active, intentional, and mutually beneficial. The relationship allows for accountability, support, and collaboration on a consistent basis and goes beyond casual meetings.

Although you want to have plenty of business relationships with the different categories provided in this book (review the categories again in Step 4 if you need to), you also want to have several EntrepreFriendships. It's a lot like in our personal lives: We may have relationships with a lot of different people who play different roles in our lives, but we tend to have a few close friendships that are more involved and supportive. This is how business relationships and EntrepreFriendships work: You'll have a lot business relationships and a few or several EntrepreFriendships.

I have a system to make this process more strategic for you. Follow this process for each person on your list with whom you want to build an EntrepreFriendship.

How to Spot a Potential EntrepreFriendship

Identifying a great potential EntrepreFriendship is a lot like identifying a great industry influencer/connector. Review the characteristics listed in Step 4 to remind you of what you're looking for in the different categories. A potential EntrepreFriend will likely have the following characteristics:

- Active in the community (online or offline)
- Friendly and supportive of others
- Devoted to building a great brand
- Connected with others or has a desire to do so
- Someone you see often (online or offline)
- Has a positive reputation
- Building a brand with integrity
- Ccommitted to personal growth and development

You also want to go with your intuition. Your intuition may also tell you who would be a great business relationship and who would be a great EntrepreFriend. Some people you meet will have great energy, and you'll feel really pumped up and excited around them. You may have a really great initial spark and have wonderful conversations. These can be signs of great EntrepreFriendship in the making. Use this connection process to help you take a great business relationship to the EntrepreFriendship level.

Business Relationship to EntrepreFriendship: The Process

There's a process to building relationships and turning those relationships into EntrepreFriendships. Building EntrepreFriendships is a process that takes time, and careful attention to intuition and the flow and vibe of the other person. When you've identified a great business relationship opportunity that you'd like to turn into an EntrepreFriendship, follow this process to help you build the EntrepreFriendship. First, though, review these tips.

Tip: When the initial meeting is at a live, in-person event and you exchange business cards, take pictures of the cards and make notes of something you want to remember. If you don't exchange business cards but you do exchange contact information, be sure to indicate

some helpful notes in the contact to help you remember where you met. Include details such as:
- What is their business?
- When and where did you meet?
- What was a highlight of your conversation?
- Did they mention anything funny or interesting?
- Why would this be a good person to follow up with?

Tip for when they haven't met you yet: If there's no initial meeting and they do not know you, you want to proceed with a heart of service. Think about how can you service and support them. Review Step 5 to determine how to connect and engage with them. Do this until you've made a connection and ultimately had an opportunity to connect via telephone or email, or in person. Once you've made a personal connection you can proceed with the following steps to build the EntrepreFriendship.

The process for building EntrepreFriendships is broken into six phases:
- Phase 1: Connect on Social Media
- Phase 2: Reach Out
- Phase 3: Get Personal
- Phase 4: Cultivate the Business Relationship
- Phase 5: Build the EntrepreFriendship
- Phase 6: Keep Communication Open and Consistent

Phase 1: Connect on Social Media
Follow and engage the new contact on social media.

Give them a shout-out on social media: "Nice to meet you. (And add a specific comment; refer to the note you made on their card.) Looking forward to connecting again soon."

Phase 2: Reach Out
Reach out to them again (one to two days after social media announcement). Send an email.

If you did not establish that you would be sending them an email or connecting with them while at the event/location where you met, you can still send an email.

If you met at an event:
- Thank them for meeting/connecting at the event.
- Comment on/compliment their work.
- Ask to connect for meet and greet.

Also include the following: "I would like to know more about your business and learn more about how you do what you do. My hope is that I can learn more about you so that I may be able to send you referrals and hear more how I can support you and your business."

If you did indicate that you would send them an email to connect further, follow the example in Step 2, Part 4.

Phase 3: Get Personal
Part 1: prep for the one-on-one meeting
It doesn't matter if you're meeting in person, over Skype, or a combination of both; preparation is necessary to make the most of the meeting. This phase can be used for any one-on-one meeting.

1. **Do the research prep work** (in Step 2 of this book) for different things to find out.
2. **Be positive.**
- What can make him/her smile?
- What are off-limits topics?

3. **Be early.** (You want to get there before them.) Consider bringing a branded gift. For example, if you have branded water bottles or notebooks, then consider bringing this for them.
4. **Be on brand with attire.**
5. **Prepare to ask interesting and meaningful questions** that create intelligent dialogue. Prepare topics to talk about prior to the meeting. (This is why doing the research is so important.) Here are some examples:
- What's your story? How did you get started?
- How did you overcome the nerves to go for your dream?

- What are you most motivated about right now?
- What feels the most challenging right now?
- What type of connections are most important right now?
  - How do they help you?
- What's working really well in your business right now?
- What type of connections do you wish to make?

Part 2: how to have the conversation

1. **Find out more about them.** (The goal is to learn more about how you can connect with them, and support and serve them.)
   - Be sure to engage in conversation around their values, goals, vision, and business needs. Get to know their business and their background. Establish a common frame of reference.
   - Find out who do they do business with, what makes them different, and how they add value.
2. **Find out how to support and serve.**
   - Be authentic (real and honest) and helpful. Find out something specific that you can help them with, such as how can you help them get clients.
   - Other examples:
     - Meet a need or solve a dilemma that they are having in their business.
     - Help them brainstorm ideas for a business obstacle.
     - Offer to help them reach a goal.
     - Share their news or info.
     - Attend or support an event or promotion they are having.
3. **Share your brand.** How can you help them see the value in what you do? Share your business with them (potential client) or ask for the referral (if it feels natural). Share a way you could use help or support. Give them an opportunity to help you.
4. **Stay in touch.** End with an invitation to get together again and follow through on any actions/suggestions discussed. Determine the best way to stay in touch. It's best to set a date while you're together to meet again, but this is not always possible.

Phase 4: Cultivate the Business Relationship
- Follow through on the thing you identified to support and serve them.

- Send a personal note or email to thank them for the one-on-one meeting.
- Suggest a time to get together again (and follow the steps for the one-on-one meeting). If you determined the time during your meeting, be sure to mention how you're looking forward to meeting together again (and include the date/time/location).
  - Consider inviting them to attend a community event or engagement.

After the initial meeting, you will follow the steps here in Phase 4 for a few rounds to cultivate and build the business relationship. You may want to do this a few times, before you progress to building an EntrepreFriendship. If after a few rounds of Phase 4, you decide that it doesn't make sense, or seem like a good fit or the right time to move up to an EntrepreFriendship with this new business relationship, then skip to Phase 6: Keep Communication Open and Consistent. If it does make sense to keep building to the level of EntrepreFriendship, then continue reading.

Real-Life Example

When I started my business in November 2014 I was the new kid on the block. I had been a makeup artist for 10 years. People knew me as that, so I had to completely rebrand my personal brand and make a lot of new connections. I was starting from scratch. Although I knew a lot of people, they didn't know me as a brand strategist. I had to build their trust in that. It was very intimating at first. I listened to a lot of negative self-talk and almost talked myself out of pursuing something I truly believed God is leading me to do.

I did a lot of inner work, prayer, and soul-searching to develop the clarity and confidence to pursue my career as a brand strategist and mentor, but it was scary. I had to build new relationships and reshape how existing connections saw me. Not a fun task to be faced with when you're just getting started in a new business! But it's one that we all have to face as we launch our businesses and continue to grow them. We can't avoid this process of making connections if we really want to make the impact that we are created to make.

So, when I started this business I created a long-term growth strategy for my brand. Part of that strategy was a lot of public speaking. I knew that by speaking as often as possible that I could spread my four core brand messages, which are to **embrace authenticity and achieve your definition of success; to build a brand and a life that embraces who you are, what you want, and the purpose for your life; to build real community; and to shine bright while you're doing it—in fact, to shine brighter in business and in life.**

I knew I could share these core messages and get people excited about what I could do for them in their business and in life, but they first needed to actually know I existed. That's why for the first several years of business the primary focus has to be on building brand awareness and building those relationships. As time goes on the focus can shift into other areas, but building relationships still needs to remain primary. So the public speaking was a win-win. Plus, I knew it would be a great way for people to get to experience the fun and natural energy I bring with me, which would help me stand out and attract my ideal clients.

Public speaking is a great way to grow your brand and make new connections. Thus, I did some research to find different opportunities to speak and came upon a really cool conference: the Blink Conference. I did some reading on the website to see what it was all about and decided it was something I'd really like to be involved in. The creators of the conference, Tash and Ike, didn't know me. They didn't know anything about me. I was basically doing a cold reach-out, and I hoped that I would get a response. And fortunately for me, Tash reached back. Although they had all of their speakers for 2015, she suggested we chat to connect. So, I was thrilled for a few reasons: (1) She responded, (2) She reached back and gave me an invitation to get to know more about her, and (3) The opportunity to support and serve was near.

We scheduled the call for a few weeks later. On the scheduled day of the call, I called her and she didn't answer. I was bummed. I felt disappointed, but before the disappointment settled in the phone rang. She called me and we chatted for nearly an hour. We had an instant connection. I knew from that first conversation that she'd be someone that I'd want to build a friendship with and someone I wanted to support. Her heart is what convinced me. She was so honest, real, and open during that call that I really wanted to act on the opportunity to help her by using my platform. So I said, "Hey, do you want to do an interview on Periscope?" She agreed.

(Periscope is a social media platform for live video streaming. For more information on how to use Periscope for building you brand, please review my Purposed Periscope Guide on my website: www. MoniqueMelton.com.)

That was the opportunity right there: I offered to support and serve her by doing an interview on Periscope that would give her an opportunity to connect with my growing community and to promote her conference. No strings attached. I wasn't looking for anything in return. I was excited to support her and excited to share what she was doing.

Fast-forward to the interview. The Periscope internet connection was probably the worst it had ever been, and we had plenty of technical difficulties, but we pressed through. During the interview while we were talking about the conference I said, "I should just come and crash your conference and Periscope it." And she replied: "Let's do it. Let's chat offline and we'll set it up."

I thought, *"Really. Did that just happen? Did I just invite myself to her conference and did she just accept? Wow!"*

After we ended the broadcast we chatted about the conference and what my role would be. I would come to the conference, interview all of the speakers, show the behind-the-scenes, and interview some of the attendees. Simple enough, right? And although I had never been an official media correspondent before, I was pumped. I knew I could handle it because cameras and I have a really cool relationship, and then you combine that with loving and being really great with connecting with people, and the result just has to be amazing.

And it may sound like I'm tooting my own horn, but the impact created from what we did with Periscope at her conference was phenomenal.

It was much more than what either one of us expected. The interviews were lively, hilarious, fun, educational, and packed with unscripted, incredible inspiration. Plus, we tripled the Blink Conference Periscope following in three days. On the second day of the conference, Tash said to me, "You have to come next year. I already put you in my budget!"

Neither one of us immediately recognized what we were doing when we agreed to invite one another into our worlds, but we were creating opportunities, building a relationship, and building our brands.

Here I was, this woman that Tash didn't even know existed, but I was I was and still am very determined to build relationships. I reached out to her and offered to support and serve her, and she reached back and gave me that opportunity. I first supported her by doing the Periscope broadcast and I could have stopped there. But I didn't.

The thing is, when you support people, you can't hold back. You have to be willing to invest in them—fully, or it just won't be as impactful. And that's what I did. Tash told me to get to the conference and that she would take care of everything else. We put everything in writing and made it official. So there was an investment there: I paid more than $500 for a plane ticket, spent four days away from my family and business, and spent several hours each day of the conference live broadcasting and pouring love and support into someone I just met. Risky, right? But isn't business about taking risk and walking it out in faith (having the hope for the best, for what is unseen—yet for what is desired)? Tash and I were both were walking by faith and it was totally worth it.

Tash and I have not only become friends in business but we are EntrepreFriends. We support one another in business and in our personal lives. She supports my business by introducing me to her community and giving me opportunities to serve them. And she's also invested in me by asking me to come and be the official Periscope correspondent for the Blink Conference 2017.

To this day, people still talk about that Periscope broadcast, and they gave such rave reviews. Really, all it was were two women taking a chance on one another and trusting God to do something amazing—and that's exactly what happened.

We built an EntrepreFriendship that is rooted in supporting and serving one another. Thus the bond and commitment to one another is real and more meaningful.

Phase 5: Build the EntrepreFriendship

Get excited. You're really close to building an EntrepreFriendship, and that's something to be excited about. So go ahead—do your happy dance. I'll wait; go ahead. This is an exciting time because—you know this already, but I'll remind you again—EntrepreFriendships are incredibly helpful and beneficial to business growth and development. You don't need a lot, but a few can really impact your life and your business in a very positive and major way. So, yes do your happy dance, because you're almost there.

First things first, though: You have to set the parameters of this more involved and mutually beneficial relationship. Up until now, things have been a lot more informal and casual, which is great. But if you're ready to take it up a notch to build a real EntrepreFriendship, you'll want to go over some important details with one another.

Setting the parameters in the relationships and establishing boundaries are the best ways to ensure a healthy and mutually beneficial EntrepreFriendship. Follow these steps to make the best of the EntrepreFriendship. It's best to do this in person, if possible. Meet in a casual or informal setting. Sometimes this may not be possible; if you're in different locations, a phone call or video meeting could work, too.

Tip: Not every great business relationship needs to go to the next level of EntrepreFriendship. If your intuition is telling you that the current business relationship is best as is, then maybe wait a little longer before pursuing the EntrepreFriendship. Ultimately the goal is to build really great relationships and a really supportive community. It's important for me to note here that sometimes EntrepreFriendships may develop organically. Sometimes, though, you may want to move things a long without waiting for it to happen more organically, so these steps will help you navigate the process of building the EntrepreFriendship. If you've completed Phase 4 at least four or five times with the same person, and you're confident this person would make a great EntrepreFriend, then this may a good time to move forward to build the EntrepreFriendship. When you're ready follow this process:

Determine the benefit of exchange

This conversation begins by thanking them for all of the time you've been able to get to know them better and help them (insert specific things you've done to support and serve them here). Tell them you'd really like to consider partnering with one another to help one another grow in business even more. Find out if they're interested in building a business relationship that is mutually supportive and aims to really support one another in business. You can mention the EntrepreFriendship or not; basically you're looking for a few good, like-minded business friends to support and serve, and to help you grow as well.

If they seem interested, then suggest the following ways you'd be interested in supporting one another. If they seem uncomfortable or uninterested, then simply thank them for their time, go back to Phase 3, and have a great one-on-one meeting.

Identify ways to support and serve one another
- Be accountability partners.
- Exchange referrals.
- Get the word out about their events.

- Be a resource for their industry.
- Exchange business info.
- Continue to support one another.
- Volunteer for each other's events and causes.
- Share social media and emails to your community.
- Publicly recommend and review one another.

Discuss the boundaries of the EntrepreFriendship

Determine if this will be formal or informal. (Will this need to be in writing or not?)

- Discuss what the benefits of the relationship will be.
- Discuss whether there will be any exclusivity or legal matters to consider.
- Determine how often you'll meet with one another.
- Discuss how and where you will share information.
- Determine a time to check in and update one another.
- Determine how you want to send and receive referrals.
- Determine and describe the ideal referrals. (This can change over time.)

For more organic EntrepreFriendships, the boundaries may look different, but the goal is to be specific about ways in which to engage in your relationship.

Additionally, these boundaries are suggestions. Yours may look very different, and may or may not be this rigid or defined. But every relationship needs boundaries and great communication, so this is a framework to consider. After you build the EntrepreFriendship then you want to make sure you proceed to keep open and consistent communication.

Phase 6: Keep Communication Open and Consistent

Always gauge and adjust the system to meet your needs and the needs of the relationship. People are complex and this is a guide, but intuition and authenticity must remain intact for this to be effective. This is why open and consistent communication is key to maintaining a great relationship. If you have conflicts or concerns, it's best to be open about them with one another. Also, maintaining consistent communication will help the relationship be more relevant and effective, because you will be in the know about how you can support and encourage one another.

Consistent can mean different things to everyone; so that's why it's best to determine how often you'll check in with one another. Remember that this is about building real relationships with a genuine desire to support one another. Always strive to operate in honesty, integrity, and mutual honor and support for one another.

Step 7: Nurture the Relationships

♥

It's not enough to build relationships and EntrepreFriendships; you have to also nurture them. The relationships will not be like your email sequence automation, which can take care of itself, without effort from all involved. Thus it's important to regularly nurture the relationship to keep it healthy and alive.

Here are a few ideas to help you do this:

Stay in touch.
Anytime you connect either in person or online, be sure to send a personal note thanking them for the meeting.

Look for ways to support and serve.
Follow through on whatever you agree to help with.

Share their good news.
If you find out that they have some really great or new information to share, simply share it on social media (if it's public information) and tag them in the post. Express your genuine excitement for them. (Don't be fake.)

Comment and engage on their social media.
When they post information on social media, avoid liking or commenting on everything, and avoid stale or artificial comments

such as "Cool." Instead, engage in the posts that resonate with you and leave meaningful comments. (Again, don't be fake.)

Be the first to support their endeavors.
When you find out that they are taking on a new project or doing something big and bold (or something small and subtle), be the first to send a personal email to congratulate them, and volunteer to help them in a specific way. For example, if you find out that they are hosting a conference, send them an email expressing how happy for them you are (again—say it with me—don't be fake) and that you'd be happy to connect them with some of your business friends who may be interested in sponsoring the event, or something else.

Check in with one another.
If they've informed you that text is an appropriate way to communicate, consider sending them a text that simply says "Wishing you a great day!" or "I know you're working really hard, so I thought I'd encourage you to keep up the great work"—something along those lines. You have to adjust what you send based on the level of the relationship.

You can also send an email with a similar vibe but a little more text. You could send something like this:

Hey, (name). I hope you're having a really great day. It was so great meeting with you (time). And I really enjoyed helping you with (however you supported and served them). Let me know if I can help you with anything else. I really think you're adding such value to the community with your hard work, and it's really amazing to support you as you do that. I hope you have a really great day and let's get together again soon. How about (time)? Talk to you soon!

Read books together.
If you're an avid book reader or you know this person loves books, then it may be a great idea to suggest reading a book together and establishing a time to chat at a determined frequency (perhaps bi-weekly) to discuss the book.

Attend events together.

This is a great way to engage and meet new people together. You can reconvene at the event and discuss the experience with one another. This helps you build shared experiences, which are the building blocks to creating great relationships.

Collaborate on projects.
Don't suggest a project collaboration on the first or second meeting, as this may be a huge turnoff. (Trust me: I've made this mistake. I can be a bit overly excited.) Instead, reserve this for after you've had a chance to get to know one another and build trust. You may want to consider doing a styled photo shoot together, or a giveaway, or hosting an event or class. The ideas are endless; just be sure to give this time to feel more natural.

Be accountability partners.
This is a lot like the "collaborate on projects," in that you want to give this more time to feel more natural. A great way to approach this is after you've meet a few times and established a nice connection, then consider asking them about what helps them stay accountable. As they share, listen for an opportunity to suggest being one another's accountability partners. If it doesn't seem like the right fit (trust your intuition), then don't force it. But if you're just feeling nervous or fearful, simply ask: "Would you be interested in being accountability partners for a couple months to see how we can help one another be more successful?"

Tip: Make a point to engage with three new connections and nurture three existing connections each day. Put it in your calendar and stick to it.

Conclusion

♥ ————————

Whew. Do you feel like you've just finished running a marathon? Okay, I've never run a marathon—but I have attempted to carry 10 bags of groceries from the garage and up a flight of stairs just to avoid making a second trip. I was tired and winded—but I felt so accomplished. That's how you may feel as you work on this process of building business relationships and EntrepreFriendships. The process may feel long, but when navigated with authenticity, humility, and honesty, the reward may be more than you can imagine. My hope is that you will use this book as an ongoing resource to help you support and serve others, and to help you grow your brand. But remember: People are complex and ever changing, so this is a guidebook—a point of reference. You will need to adjust and rely on intuition, connection, and feedback. This book gives you great tools for getting started in building and nurturing the different business relationships.

But it doesn't stop here. Why not tell a friend about this book—maybe a potential EntrepreFriend? It will give you both an opportunity to connect and build that relationship. Can you think of someone you'd like to build a business relationship with or even an EntrepreFriendship? This book could make for a great introduction.

And I want to hear from you! I want to know how you're experiencing this book and if the strategies are working for you. I want to know your ups and downs, and help you make the most out of the time and money you spent on this book, so please don't be a stranger. (Don't be creepy, either. Creepy is not good, but do be sure to reach out and let me know your thoughts on the book.)

Remember: We were born to connect with others. We weren't meant to navigate life alone. And even though relationships can seem like a whole lot of work, they also bring so much fulfillment to our lives. The same is true with business relationships. It may seem scary or intimidating to reach out to complete strangers, because that fear of rejection is so loud that you can hardly concentrate, but when you drown it out with hope and you act in faith, you will soon realize that the fear was simply an obstacle standing in between you and what you really want. This is why faith is so important in life and in business.

A faith-based business—a business that relies on stepping out of the comfort zone and into the unknown zone—is one that will always go further and achieve more than a fear-based, comfort zone–based business. It's never fun to risk embarrassment or rejection. Those are things that really aren't meant to be enjoyed, but they also are a part of the process of getting to next level. But if you allow those fears to hold you back from taking the risk of building real and meaningful relationships, then you have a lot more to lose than that temporary feeling of embarrassment or rejection, which may never happen or happen as badly as you anticipate.

Staying in your comfort zone and refusing to take the risk of building real and meaningful relationships also means you're risking never achieving your dreams. You're risking living a life in which you'll one day look back and wish you had only taken that step—that scary, uncertain step. The possibilities are limitless, if only you can lose grip of the fear and hold tight to the faith.

Be encouraged as you continue your journey in life to walk in more faith and overcome more fear, one day and one relationship at a time.

Appendix

♥

The activities here are to help you with some of the information discussed in this book. These activities can help you with understanding your core values, understating yourself as person, and much more. They'll be most helpful to you if you complete them prior to networking. Remember: More guidance can be found in the *Building Connections* chart; my book *Threads Unraveled*; *the Purposed Periscope guide*; and the *Casting the Vision Guide,* all available on my website (www.MoniqueMelton.com).

Core Values Activity
Directions: Using the space provided below, make a list of five to 10 of your all-time favorite brands. Review their websites, and search for their mission and core values (or what you perceive them to be, if they are not clearly listed). Using the space provided, study the core values of each of the brands and indicate the core values that resonate with you the most. Lastly, complete the information listed below about each of the brands.

List the brands here: (You can include companies, entertainers, or people.)

List the core values here that resonate with you:

Why do these values resonate with you?

Do you want to incorporate any of these values in your brand?

What tone of voice do you notice of the brands you listed? (How do they say what they say? In other words, are they authoritative, humorous, serious, professional, playful, sarcastic, etc.?)

What are the personalities of the brand? (What adjectives would you use to describe the personality?)

What are your core values for your brand?

What will you be known for upholding/standing firm in your business?

What will you always strive to do?

What will strive to never do?

Understanding "You" Activity

Directions: Before you can get to the work of building meaningful relationships, you have to start with you. That's why I wrote my book *Threads Unraveled: Embrace Who You Are, What You Want, and the Purpose for Your Life*: to help you start with "you." The more you know about yourself, the more confident and comfortable you can be in building those relationships. And understanding who you are and what makes your heart sing is key to attracting the people you desire to work with in your business. People want to connect with real people. When you show up and are real, authentic, and true, then a real and lasting connection can be made. But before that, you have to know who you are, tap into your best authentic-self, and really show up in your business with confidence, clarity, and purpose.

Take a few minutes to honestly answer these questions yourself and for more in-depth exploration, please check out Turn-up Your Bright: Embrace who you are, what you want and the purpose for your life. The more focus you can develop in your personal identity, the better. This activity has two sections, so please take your time to complete both.

Take a few minutes to honestly answer these questions about yourself. For more in-depth exploration, please check out *Threads Unraveled*. The more focus you can develop in your personal identity, the better. This activity has two sections, so please take your time to complete both.

Section 1: Define Your Identity
Use these questions to help you begin exploring who you are as a person.

1. Who are you?
   a. How do you define your identity?

      i. What metaphors describe you?

      ii. What type of songs would you dance to all night?

      iii. What have people told you about yourself that you know to be true?

2. How often do you encourage, uplift, and motivate yourself? Can you do more?

3. Do a personal analysis of yourself.
   a. What are your top five to six strengths, weaknesses, opportunities, and threats?

   b. What are your distinct gifts and talents that come very easily to you?

   c. Who did you dream of being when you were younger?

   d. What do you really care about?

      i. What ideas are already out there that have traction?
         • Which ones do you dislike? Why?

      ii. What types of posts on social media get you pumped up?

      iii. What breaks your heart?

      iv. What do you want to make a stance on?

e. What are your core beliefs? What do you know to be true for your life?

f. What do you believe in more than anything?

g. What are your convictions? What are you unwilling to undermine or settle on?

4. What do you want for yourself in life?
   a. What do you want most in life?

   b. What type of life do you want to live?

   c. What would "having it all" mean to you?

   d. What are you willing to give up to get it?

   e. Who do you want to impress?

f. What are you willing to look silly doing?

g. What are willing to bleed, sweat, and cry to have?

5. Why are you doing what you do?

a. What motivates you to keep pressing on, even when it's challenging?

b. Whose life do you really want to impact and why?

6. What does living authentically mean to you?

a. How can being your best authentic-self impact your life?

b. What type of thoughts do you play in your mind?
   • Do they make you feel good about yourself?

7. What do you believe for yourself more than anything?

8. If you could have anything right now in your life, what would it be?

Section 2: Set the Vision

Use these questions to help you determine the vision for your brand and what you're looking to accomplish long term. For more guidance in how to take your vision and determine clear steps to take accomplish your goals, please check out the guide *Casting the Vision* on my website (www.MoniqueMelton.com) in the "Shop" section.

1. Overall: What is your specific vision for yourself?

2. What are your long-term goals for brand?

3. What's that one really big, extravagant, outrageous goal that you want to accomplish?

4. What would it mean to you to achieve this really big goal you mentioned in #3?

5. Are you pursuing this goal or are you running from it? Why?

6. What would success look like in your career with your company?

7. What limitations and weaknesses (consider thought processes and fears) are you most aware of at this time that may be hindering you from reaching your goals? (What areas need improvement?)

8. Where do you want to see your interaction in the community?

9. How many years do you want to actively be working in the business?

10. What are you trying to achieve over the next six to 12 months? You can break this up into three specific goals and then outline specific steps to take to accomplish this goal.

These two sections are just a tip of the iceberg for self-discovery, so be please be sure to dive deeper with my book, *Threads Unraveled*, and take action with the *Casting the Vision Guide*.

If you want to explore any of the information further, please contact me. I work with passionate entrepreneurs and women in business with private sessions, workshops, speaking events/conferences, group courses, and masterminds, so I'm sure I have something to support you. You can subscribe to my mailing list and learn more about my services at www.MoniqueMelton.com. Thank you for investing in your business by reading this book to help you build business relationships. Remember to support and serve, and be consistent. I wish you much success. If this book has helped you in any way, please reach out and let me know by contacting pr@MoniqueMelton.com, and be sure to use the hashtag #EntrepreFriendships to share the love!

Thank you!

#EntrepreFriendships

Buy your Support and Serve products at MoniqueMelton.com.

Life

IS

better

WITH

friends.

Made in the USA
Lexington, KY
10 August 2016